A Party Bear

Written by Ben Raker

Illustrated by Wendy Edelson

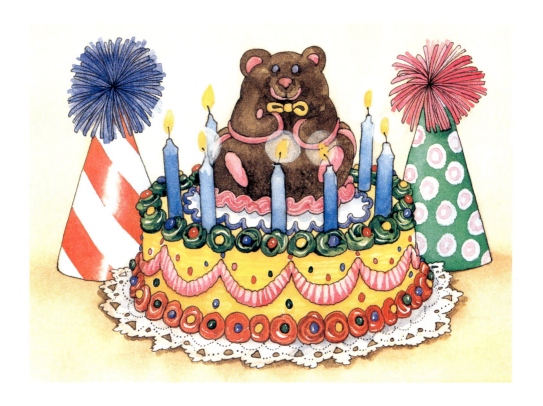

Rabbit has a friend.

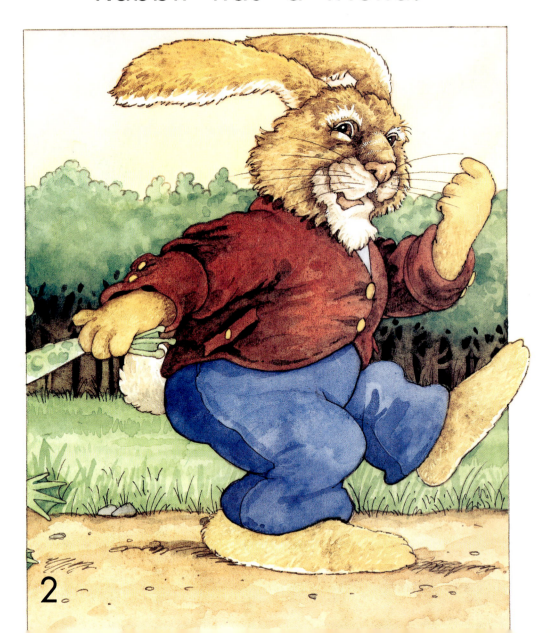

Frog has a friend.

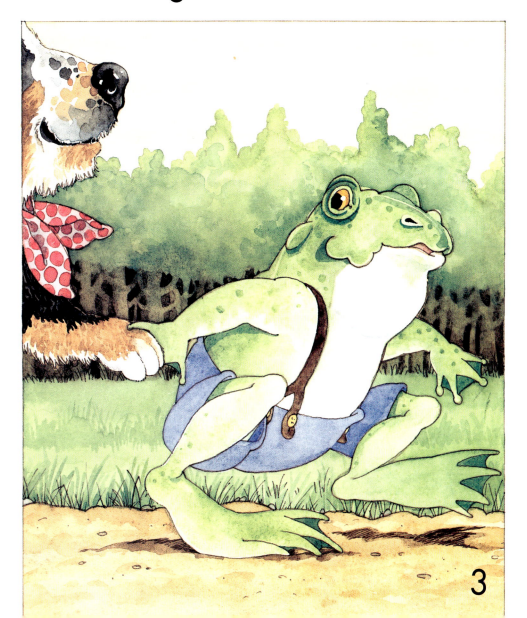

Dog has a friend.

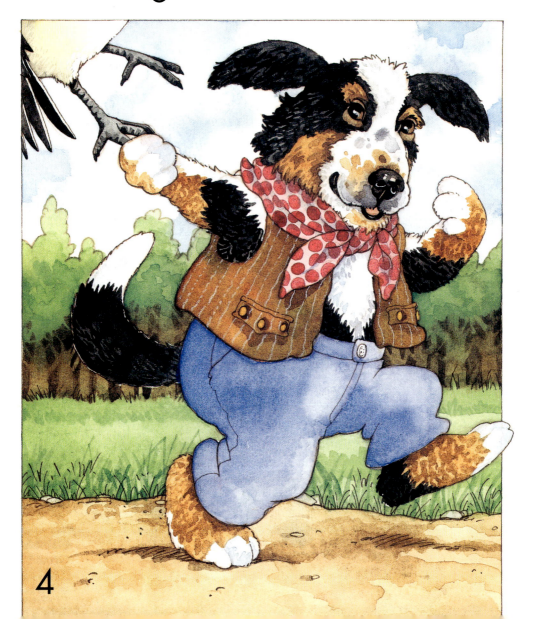

Bird has a friend.

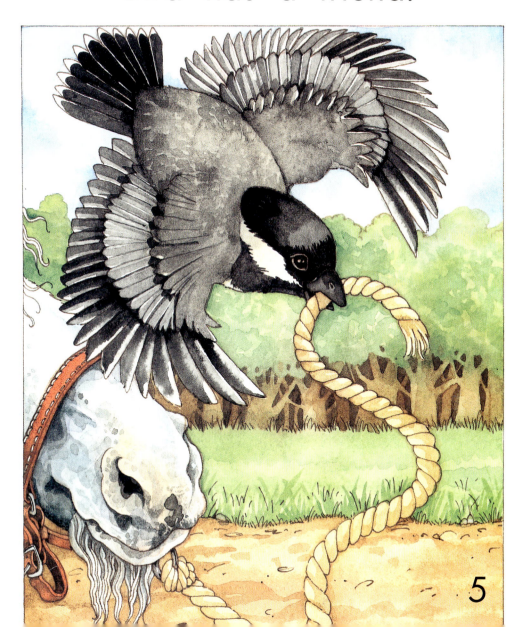

Horse has a friend.

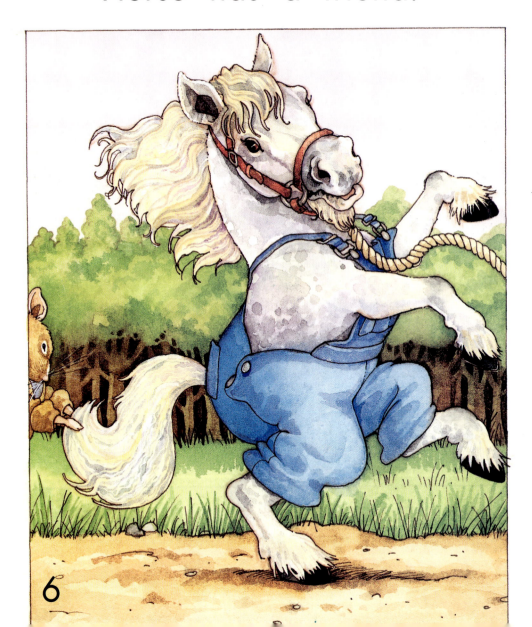

Mouse has a friend.

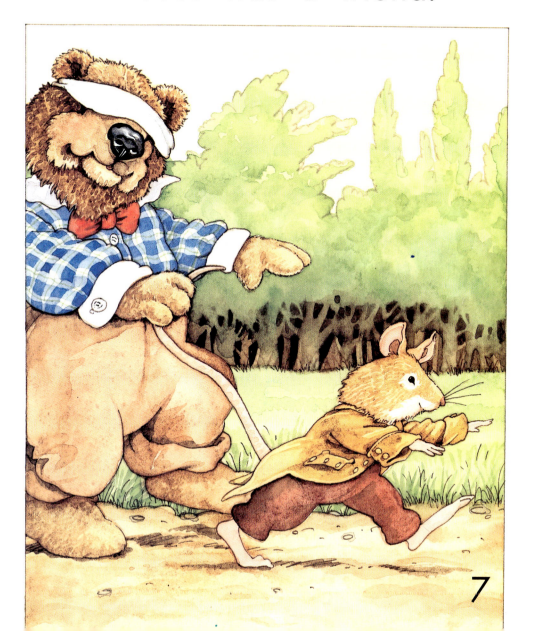

Happy birthday, Bear!